DONATED BY MS. MARGARET SC...

IMMANUEL LUTHERAN SCHOOL
SCHOEN MEMORIAL LIBRARY

MAR 3 1 2009

S0-AYQ-296

IMMANUEL LUTHERAN SCHOOL
SCHOEN MEMORIAL LIBRARY

AD 210 #2	DATE DUE	
AD 280 #2		
My 50 9 ½		
My 12 0 9 2		

2167 HC

523.6   Graham, Ian

GRA
              Comets and asteroids
[jr]   [Discovering Space]

MAR 3 1 2009 18.95

DISCOVERING Space

COMETS AND ASTEROIDS

Ian Graham

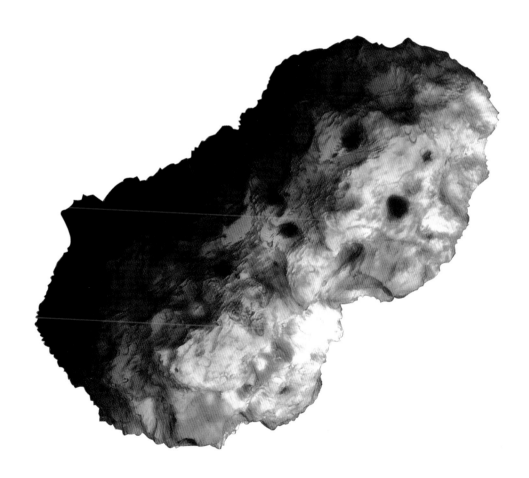

A⁺
Smart Apple Media

Published by Smart Apple Media
2140 Howard Drive West
North Mankato, MN 56003

Created by Q2A Media
Series Editor: Honor Head
Designers: Diksha Khatri, Ashita Murgai
Picture Researchers: Lalit Dalal, Jyoti Sachdev

Picture credits
t: top, b: bottom, l: left, r: right, m: middle, c: center
Cover images: Nasa: tl, Science Photo Library/ Photolibrary: tr, b,
Small images: Nasa/ JPL-Caltech: ml, Michael Puerzer/ Istockphoto: mr, Sebastian Kaulitzki/ Shutterstock: mc
Science Photo Library/ Photolibrary: 4b, 5t, 7t, 8b, 9b, 19t, 22–23 (background), 23t, 25t, 27t, William Attard McCarthy:
4–5 (background), Photo Researchers, Inc./ Photolibrary: 6b, 22b, The Bridgeman Art Library/ Photolibrary: 7b,
Roger Ressmeyer/ Corbis: 9t, Nasa/ JPL/ UMD: 10–11 (background), 20b, Nasa/ JPL-Caltech: 10b, 13t, 16b, 17t, Nasa/ JPL: 12b,
Nasa: 13b, 21t, 21b, ESA/ AOES Medialab: 15t, ESA: 14b, 15b, Nasa/ JPL-Caltech/R. Hurt (SSC): 16–17 (background),
NEAR Project: 18b, Oxford Scientific Films/ Photolibrary: 24b, 25b, Sebastian Kaulitzki/ Shutterstock: 26b,
Stephan Hoerold/ Istockphoto: 27b.

Copyright © 2008 Smart Apple Media.
International copyright reserved in all countries.
No part of this book may be reproduced in any form without written permission from the publisher.

Printed in China

Library of Congress Cataloging-in-Publication Data

Graham, Ian, 1953–
Comets and asteroids / by Ian Graham.
p. cm. — (Discovering space)
Includes index.
ISBN 978-1-59920-074-3
1. Comets—Juvenile literature. 2. Asteroids—Juvenile literature. I. Title.

QB721.5.G73 2007
523.6—dc22   2007007532

First Edition

9 8 7 6 5 4 3 2 1

Contents

Space rocks

In addition to the planets, there are a countless number of smaller objects orbiting the sun. These range in size from tiny specks of dust to huge rocks. There are also giant snowballs in space.

Leftover chunks

The planets and moons were made from a giant cloud of gas, rock, and ice swirling around the newly formed sun. But not all of the cloud was used up. A lot of chunks of rock and ice were leftover and many of these pieces are still flying around in space.

Boulders of all shapes and sizes fly through the **solar system.**

Spotlight on
space

Rocks flying through space are called meteoroids or asteroids. The only difference between them is their size. Meteoroids are space rocks that are up to several feet across. Bigger rocks are called asteroids.

Comets are giant balls of ice and rock, like snowballs in space.

Most of the pieces of rock and ice that fly through space are far too small for us to see among the stars.

Crash or burn

Rocks from space often crash into planets and moons. Earth's **atmosphere** protects us from most of them. The smallest rocks get hot as they plunge into the atmosphere and many of them burn up. When rocks hit a planet or moon without an atmosphere, they crash into the surface and make craters. Earth's moon is covered with these craters.

Comets—ice in space

Every few years, a strange fuzzy ball of light appears in the sky. It often has a long tail. In the ancient world, these unexpected visitors from space caused fear and panic. Today, we know what they are—they are called comets.

Space mountains

A comet is a mountain of ice and rock in **orbit** around the sun. Most of the time, comets are too far away to be seen from Earth. But when they get close to the sun and heat up, they change into a bright ball with a long tail.

Comet facts

Comet		Appears every
Encke	▶	3 years, 4 months
Tempel-Tuttle	▶	33 years
Halley's comet	▶	76 years
Hale-Bopp	▶	2,400 years
Kohoutek	▶	75,000 years
comet West	▶	500,000 years

A comet looks so bright because the dust it gives off reflects sunlight.

Comet tails

When a comet is heated up by sunlight, some of its ice changes into gas. Gas and dust flying off the comet form a cloud around it called a coma. The gas and dust also stretch out into a tail. Sometimes there are two tails— a faint blue tail of gas and a brighter dust tail.

Gas and dust from a comet are swept back into a tail.

Spotlight on
space

Comets come from two streams of icy objects—the Kuiper belt and the Oort cloud. The Kuiper belt is at the outer edge of the solar system. The Oort cloud is farther away.

This eighteenth-century picture shows how excited people were to see a comet.

Halley's comet

The most famous comet is Halley's comet.
It appears in the sky every 76 years. When
it last appeared in 1986, a fleet of spacecraft—
including one called *Giotto*—was launched to
meet the comet and study it up close.

Regular visitor

Halley's comet is named after the
astronomer Edmond Halley. He saw
the comet in 1682 and figured out
that it was the same comet that had
been seen in 1531 and 1607. Records
of Halley's comet have been found
going back more than 2,000 years.

Giotto was one of five **space probes**
sent to meet Halley's comet.

Giotto mission		
Launched	▶	July 2, 1985
Flew past Halley's comet	▶	March 13, 1986
Distance from Halley's comet	▶	370 miles (596 km)
End of mission	▶	July 23, 1992

Giotto's photographs show jets of gas flying out of the sunlit side of Halley's comet.

Giotto had to fly into the dust coming off Halley's comet. The dust can cause a lot of damage, so the front of the spacecraft was covered with a metal shield. _Giotto_ was hit by dust more than 12,000 times.

Dusty and crusty

Giotto's pictures of Halley's comet show that it has a **nucleus,** which is about nine miles (15 km) long and up to six miles (10 km) wide. The nucleus is made of ice mixed with dark, dusty material. The comet is covered by a thin crust of this dark material.

Halley's comet is bright enough to see in the sky without a telescope.

Deep Impact

Scientists wanted to know what a comet is like inside. They built a spacecraft called *Deep Impact* that made a hole in a comet that was flying through space.

Collision course

The *Deep Impact* spacecraft carried a large piece of metal, called an impactor, weighing 816 pounds (370 kg). As *Deep Impact* flew toward a comet called Tempel 1, it let go of the impactor so that it would collide with the comet. The spacecraft's cameras and instruments recorded what happened next.

Deep Impact mission

Launched	▶	January 12, 2005
Impactor released	▶	July 3, 2005
Impactor hit comet	▶	July 4, 2005
End of mission	▶	August 2005

The impactor from *Deep Impact* flies toward comet Tempel 1.

A flash of light

Comet Tempel 1 was discovered in 1867 by the German astronomer Wilhelm Tempel. The comet orbits the sun every $5\frac{1}{2}$ years.

When the impactor from *Deep Impact* hit the sunlit side of comet Tempel 1, there was a brilliant flash of light as sunlight bounced off the cloud of particles that was thrown into space from the crash. The particles included dust and ice. The comet was only held together by **gravity**, so it was easy to make a hole in it.

The camera on *Deep Impact* watches as its impactor crashes into Tempel 1.

Collecting stardust

In 1999, a space probe was sent to meet a comet, collect dust particles from it, and bring them back to Earth. No one had ever tried such a daring space mission to study a comet before.

Wild-2

The comet chosen for this mission was Wild-2. It orbits the sun every six years and five months. The spacecraft, called *Stardust*, was carefully aimed to meet Wild-2 as it sped through space.

Stardust mission

Launched	▶	February 7, 1999
Flew past comet Wild-2	▶	January 2, 2004
Returned to Earth	▶	January 15, 2006
Total distance traveled	▶	2 billion miles (3.2 billion km)

Stardust was hit by thousands of dust particles as it flew through space toward the comet.

Stardust collected comet dust by catching it in a material called aerogel. Aerogel is a spongy jelly. When a dust particle flies into it, the aerogel gently slows the particle down, so it will not be damaged.

Wild-2 was not discovered until 1978.

Return to Earth

When *Stardust* finished collecting dust from Wild-2, it headed back to Earth. As it passed Earth, it dropped a **capsule** containing the dust. Parachutes helped the capsule land safely. Space scientists are now studying the comet dust. Meanwhile, the *Stardust* spacecraft is still in space. It may be sent to visit another comet.

Stardust's capsule sits on the ground after returning from space.

Heat shield

Parachute straps

Landing on a comet

The *Rosetta* space mission will try to learn more about comets by landing a small probe on one. The spacecraft began its journey in 2004. It has to travel so far that it will not reach the comet until 2014.

Orbit and land

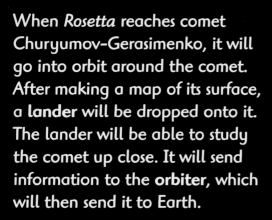

When *Rosetta* reaches comet Churyumov-Gerasimenko, it will go into orbit around the comet. After making a map of its surface, a **lander** will be dropped onto it. The lander will be able to study the comet up close. It will send information to the **orbiter**, which will then send it to Earth.

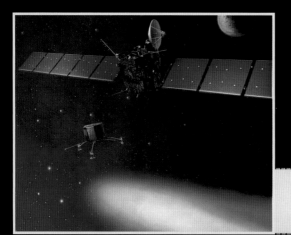

Rosetta mission

Launched	▶	March 2, 2004
1st Earth flyby	▶	March 2005
Mars flyby	▶	February 2007
2nd Earth flyby	▶	November 2007
Asteroid Steins flyby	▶	September 2008
3rd Earth flyby	▶	November 2009
Asteroid Lutetia flyby	▶	July 2010
Arrival at comet	▶	May 2014
Landing on comet	▶	November 2014

The lander from the *Rosetta* will follow comet Churyumov-Gerasimenko.

Rosetta was going to visit a comet called Wirtanen. But the rocket that was going to launch the spacecraft had an accident, and the launch was delayed. The mission was changed and *Rosetta* was sent to visit a different comet called Churyumov-Gerasimenko.

Rosetta swoops over the comet.

Rosetta's lander will fire a harpoon into the comet so that the lander does not float away into space.

Flight path

Rosetta is set to follow a very complicated flight path. It will fly past Earth three times and once past Mars. It will do this because the rocket that launched it was not powerful enough to send it straight to the comet. Instead, it will use gravity from Earth and Mars to boost its speed. Each time it passes Earth or Mars, the pull of the planet's gravity will help it go faster, building up the speed it needs to reach the comet.

Asteroids

Millions of chunks of rock orbit the sun. They are called asteroids. Even though some of them are hundreds of miles wide, they are so far away that they cannot be seen without a powerful telescope.

Where are they?

Most asteroids are in the space between the planets Mars and Jupiter. This is called the **asteroid belt**. There are asteroids in other places, too. Trojan asteroids are in the same orbit as Jupiter and there are asteroids that come close to Earth.

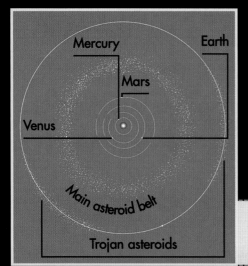

The biggest asteroids

Ceres was once known as the biggest asteroid in the solar system. Then, in 2006, astronomers decided that Ceres should be called a dwarf planet.

Name		Size across the middle
Ceres	▶	584 miles (940 km)
Vesta	▶	335.5 miles (540 km)
Pallas	▶	326 miles (525 km)
Hygeia	▶	267 miles (430 km)
Interamnia	▶	202 miles (325 km)
Davida	▶	202 miles (325 km)

Space probes flying to the far planets have to go through the asteroid belt.

Mathilde is an asteroid that measures about 36.5 miles (59 km) wide.

Spotlight on
space

Asteroids are not all the same. Some of them are very dark because they contain a lot of carbon. Some are made of light-colored rock. Others are shiny, because they are made of metal.

Changing direction

Asteroids sometimes change direction. They might be hit by another asteroid, or they can be pulled by the gravity of a nearby planet. Sometimes when this happens, an asteroid flies out of the asteroid belt and closer to the sun. These asteroids are called near-Earth asteroids.

NEAR-Shoemaker

Asteroids are hard to study because they are so far away and difficult to see. Even through a powerful telescope, they look like tiny bright pinpoints moving among the stars. To see an asteroid up close, scientists have to send a space probe.

Visiting Eros

The *NEAR-Shoemaker* space probe was sent to study the asteroid Eros. It spent a year orbiting Eros. Then, to end the mission, the probe slowly descended and landed on Eros. It is the first spacecraft to land on an asteroid.

NEAR-Shoemaker mission

Launched	▶	February 17, 1996
Flew past Mathilde	▶	June 27, 1997
Flew past Earth	▶	January 23, 1998
Flew past Eros	▶	December 23, 1998
Went into orbit around Eros	▶	February 14, 2000
Landed on Eros	▶	February 12, 2001
End of mission	▶	February 28, 2001

This asteroid is called Eros. It was the first near-Earth asteroid to be discovered.

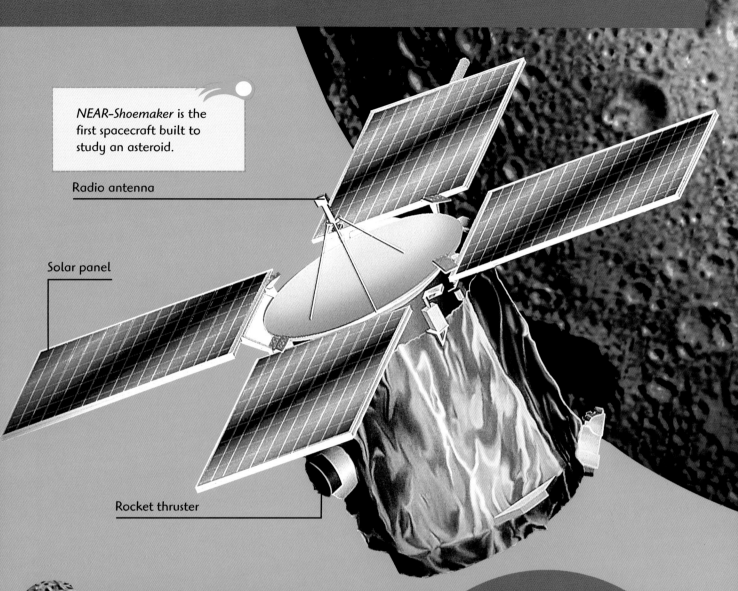

NEAR-Shoemaker is the first spacecraft built to study an asteroid.

Radio antenna

Solar panel

Rocket thruster

Surprise, surprise!

Scientists were amazed that *NEAR-Shoemaker* found so much dust and so many rocks on the asteroid. The scientists had thought Eros's gravity was too weak to hold onto anything. They found that most of the large rocks came from Eros itself. The rocks had been thrown out of a crater that was made when a meteoroid hit Eros one billion years ago.

Spotlight on space

Eros is a near-Earth asteroid. It travels around the sun every 643 days at a speed of about 54,000 miles (87,000 km) per hour. That is more than 100 times faster than a jet airplane!

Space dust

Even the smallest pieces of dust and grit flying around in space can be dangerous. These pieces are called **micrometeoroids**. They can cause a lot of damage, so the people who design spacecraft need to know about them.

Punching holes

Micrometeoroids are tiny pieces of rock and metal from asteroids and comets, and they travel very fast. Spacecraft have shields to stop micrometeoroids from punching holes in them. Some spacecraft have instruments that count the number of times they are hit by micrometeoroids. This helps scientists learn more about these small pieces of space dust and find out how many are flying around in space.

Micrometeoroid facts

Size	▶	smaller than a grain of sand
Weight	▶	less than 1 gram
Speed	▶	up to 50 miles (80 km) per second

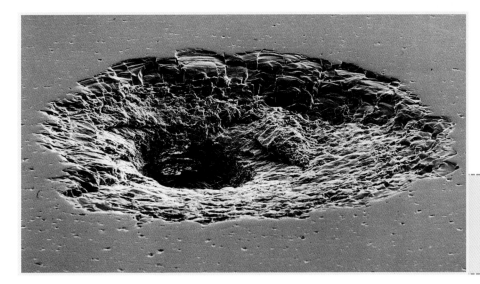

This looks like a large crater, but it is really a close-up photograph of a tiny hole made by a micrometeoroid.

Radiators

Soyuz spacecraft

Solar panels

Laboratory

The **International Space Station** has shields to protect it from micrometeoroids.

Spotlight on
space

There are many millions of tiny pieces of matter flying around in space. Not all of them are micrometeoroids. Some are flakes of metal and paint from old rockets and spacecraft.

Thousands of hits

In 1984, a spacecraft covered with pieces of different types of materials was launched into space. It was left there for nearly six years to see what would happen to it. The spacecraft was called the *LDEF* (the *Long Duration Exposure Facility*). By the time it was brought back to Earth in 1990, it had been hit 20,000 times.

The *LDEF* spacecraft showed how many times a spacecraft could be hit by space dust.

Shooting stars

On a clear night, you might see a bright streak of light in the sky. It appears and disappears in a second. This is called a shooting star, but it is not a star at all.

Hot rocks

When a meteoroid flies into Earth's atmosphere, it heats up until it glows. The rock becomes so hot that it changes into gas, or **vaporizes**. It only takes a moment for a small piece of rock to vaporize completely.

Meteor showers

Shower name		When seen each year
Quadrantids	▶	January 3–4
Lyrids	▶	April 21–22
Perseids	▶	August 11–12
Orionids	▶	October 21–22
Taurids	▶	November 4–5
Leonids	▶	November 17–18
Geminids	▶	December 13–14

Meteors usually start glowing about 62 miles (100 km) above the ground.

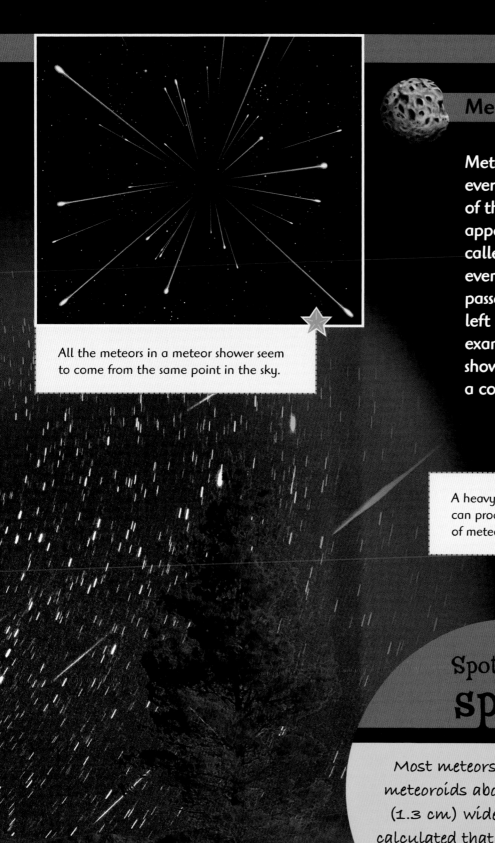

Meteor shower

Meteors fly through the sky every night. At certain times of the year, many meteors appear together in what are called meteor showers. These events happen when Earth passes through a trail of dust left behind by a comet. For example, the Perseids meteor shower in August is caused by a comet called Swift-Tuttle.

All the meteors in a meteor shower seem to come from the same point in the sky.

A heavy meteor shower can produce thousands of meteors an hour.

Spotlight on
space

Most meteors are produced by meteoroids about a half an inch (1.3 cm) wide. Scientists have calculated that about 100 million meteoroids plunge into Earth's atmosphere every day.

Meteorites

Only the smallest space rocks burn up in the air. Bigger rocks fall all the way down to Earth's surface. A space rock that lands on Earth is called a meteorite. Hundreds of thousands of **meteorites** fall to Earth every year.

Big rocks, small rocks

A meteorite can be as small as the period that ends this sentence or as big as a house. Luckily, most meteorites are very small. The biggest meteorites rarely fall to Earth, perhaps only once every one million years.

The largest meteorite ever found on Earth is at Hoba West, Namibia in Africa. The meteorite is made of iron and nickel.

Amazing meteorites

Name	
Hoba West	▶ the biggest meteorite ever found: 66 tons (60 t)
Williamette	▶ the biggest meteorite in the United States: 15 tons (14 t)
Orgueil	▶ contains carbon and diamond dust
Sayh al Uhaymir	▶ a meteorite from the moon
ALH84001	▶ a meteorite from Mars
Heat Shield Rock	▶ a meteorite found on Mars by the rover vehicle, *Opportunity*

A meteorite heats up, glows, and burns as it plunges into Earth's atmosphere.

Rock history

Meteorites may have been flying through space for billions of years before they landed on Earth. Scientists study them because they contain information about the history of the solar system. Some meteorites come from the moon or Mars. They were sent into space by rocks crashing into the surface of the moon or Mars.

Spotlight on
space

There are three types of meteorites. Most meteorites are made of rock and are called stony meteorites. About one meteorite in every 16 is made of iron. The rest are a mixture of stone and iron called stony-irons.

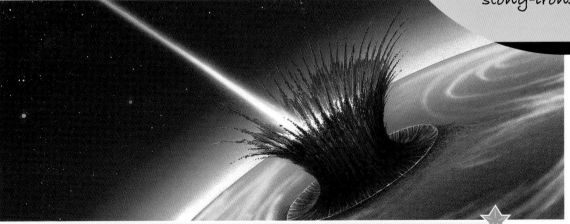

When the biggest meteorites hit Earth, they make huge craters in the ground.

Colliding with Earth

Earth has been hit by meteorites many times in the past, and it may be hit again in future. Scientists are always scanning the sky, searching for any asteroids or comets that might be on a collision course with Earth.

Global disaster

Although it is very unlikely, if a giant comet or asteroid hit Earth, it would affect the whole planet. Enormous waves would wash over much of the planet. So much soil and rock would be thrown into the atmosphere that the sun would be blocked for months.

In the past, a massive asteroid crashing into Earth may have looked like this.

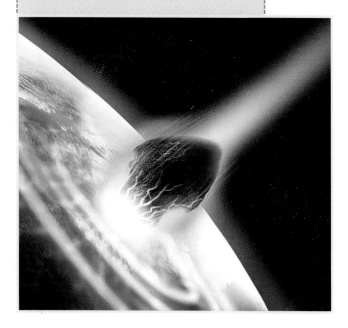

Earth impact facts

Object size	Impact on Earth
Up to 30 feet (9 m)	explodes harmlessly in the air
165 feet (50 m)	explodes in the air and causes damage on the ground
330 feet (101 m)	hits the ground and causes serious damage
0.6 miles (1 km)	massive destruction affects the whole Earth
6 miles (10 km)	few people survive anywhere on Earth

Entire forests in Siberia were flattened when a meteorite exploded above the ground in 1908.

Spotlight on
space

Several organizations watch the sky for any large objects that might be coming toward Earth. They include Spaceguard, NEAT (Near-Earth Asteroid Tracking), and LONEOS (the Lowell Observatory Near-Earth Object Search).

Saving Earth

If a comet or asteroid is seen heading for Earth, it can be pushed off course by a rocket or by exploding a powerful bomb near it. To do this successfully, scientists need to know what comets and asteroids are made of and how hard or crumbly they are. Space missions like *Rosetta* are supplying them with this vital information.

This crater was made in Arizona 50,000 years ago, when a meteorite weighing up to 330,500 tons (300,000 t) hit the ground. The crater measures 3,937 feet (1,200 m) wide and 656 feet (200 m) deep.

Time line

240 B.C.
The first recorded appearance of the comet that is now known as Halley's comet.

1682
English astronomer Edmond Halley sees the comet that is now known as Halley's comet.

1798
For the first time, scientists measure the height of meteors flying above the ground.

1801
Italian astronomer Giuseppe Piazzi is the first to discover and identify an asteroid; he called it Ceres. In 2006, astronomers decide that Ceres is a dwarf planet.

1802
A second asteroid, Pallas, is discovered.

1803
Scientists learn what meteorites are.

1804
A third asteroid, Juno, is discovered.

1807
A fourth asteroid, Vesta, is discovered.

1826
Biela's comet is discovered.

1845
A fifth asteroid, Astraea, is discovered.

1852
Biela's comet appears in the sky, but it is never seen again.

1858
Donati's comet appears.

1866
Scientists discover that meteor showers are caused by dust from comets.

1892
Photographs of a comet are taken for the first time.

1898
The first asteroid to come close to Earth is discovered. This near-Earth asteroid is called Eros.

1908
A comet or asteroid falls in Siberia and causes widespread damage. This is called the The Tunguska Event.

1949
American astronomer Fred Whipple suggests that comets are like dirty snowballs—a mixture of ice, dust, and bits of rock.

1950
Dutch astronomer Jan Oort suggests that comets come from a swarm of icy objects about one **light-year** from the sun. It becomes known as the Oort cloud.

1965
Comet Ikeya-Seki is bright enough to be seen in daylight.

1976
A bright comet, comet West, appears in the sky.

1984
The *Long Duration Exposure Facility (LDEF)* is launched to study the damaging effects of micrometeoroids on spacecraft.

1985
The *Giotto* space probe is launched to photograph Halley's comet.

1986
Giotto successfully takes close-up photographs of Halley's comet.

1990
The *Long Duration Exposure Facility (LDEF)* is brought back to Earth by the space shuttle.

1992
The *Giotto* space probe flies past comet Grigg-Skjellerup.

Comet Shoemaker-Levy 9 breaks into pieces as it passes the giant planet Jupiter.

1993
On its way to Jupiter, the *Galileo* space probe photographs the asteroid Ida and discovers that it has its own moon, Dactyl.

1994
The pieces of comet Shoemaker-Levy 9 crash into Jupiter.

1996
The *NEAR-Shoemaker* space probe is launched to visit an asteroid called Eros.

1997
NEAR-Shoemaker flies past an asteroid called Mathilde.

1999
The *Stardust* space probe is launched to visit comet Wild-2.

2000
NEAR-Shoemaker goes into orbit around the asteroid Eros.

2001
NEAR-Shoemaker lands on the asteroid Eros.

2002
The *Stardust* space probe flies past an asteroid called Annefrank.

2003
The *Rosetta* space probe is launched to visit comet Churyumov-Gerasimenko.

2004
Stardust successfully collects particles from comet Wild-2.

2006
Stardust returns to Earth with comet particles.

Astronomers identify a new type of object in the solar system, the dwarf planet. The largest asteroid, Ceres, and several other objects are now called dwarf planets.

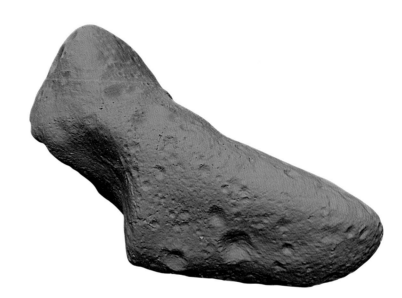

Glossary

aerogel A spongy jelly used to catch dust particles in space.

asteroids Large pieces of rock, smaller than a dwarf planet, in orbit around the sun.

asteroid belt The area between Mars and Jupiter where most asteroids are found.

astronomer A scientist who studies astronomy.

atmosphere The gas around a planet or moon. Earth's atmosphere is made of a mixture of gases called air.

capsule A small spacecraft or a compartment inside a spacecraft.

carbon An element found in some asteroids and meteorites.

comets Balls of ice and dust in orbit around the sun.

dwarf planet A large round object that orbits the sun but is not big enough to be called a planet.

gravity An invisible force that pulls things toward each other. Earth's gravity keeps us on the ground. The sun's gravity holds the planets, comets, and asteroids in their orbits.

International Space Station A large spacecraft where astronauts live while they explore space.

Kuiper belt Space beyond the planet Neptune where many icy objects orbit the sun. The dwarf planet Pluto may be a Kuiper belt object, instead of a dwarf planet.

lander A spacecraft that lands on a planet, moon, comet, or asteroid.

light-year Unit of measurement. One light-year is the distance light travels in one year, or 5.8 trillion miles (9.5 trillion km).

meteors Bright streaks of light in the sky caused by a meteoroid entering Earth's atmosphere and burning up.

meteor showers Many meteors that seem to come from the same point in the sky. The showers are caused by Earth passing through a trail of dust that is left behind by a comet.

meteorite A meteoroid that survives its journey through Earth's atmosphere and hits the ground.

meteoroids Pieces of dust or rock in orbit around the sun. Meteoroids bigger than about 33 feet (10 m) wide are called asteroids.

micrometeoroids Tiny pieces of rock or dust flying around in space.

near-Earth asteroids Big chunks of rock flying around the solar system in an orbit that brings them close to Earth.

nucleus The ball of ice and dust that forms a comet.

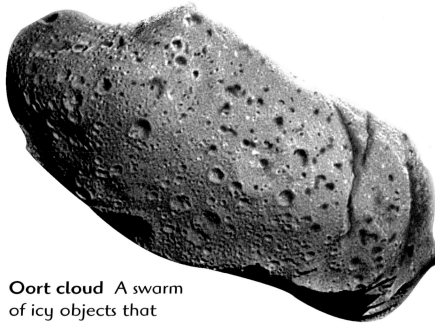

Oort cloud A swarm of icy objects that surround the solar system far beyond the farthest planet. Comets are thought to come from the Oort cloud.

orbit To travel around the sun, a moon, or a planet.

orbiter A spacecraft that flies around—or orbits—a planet, moon, comet, or asteroid.

solar system The sun, planets, moons, and other objects that orbit the sun, traveling through space together.

space probes Unmanned spacecraft sent from Earth to explore part of the solar system.

space station A spacecraft that stays in space for months or years and is visited by a series of crews.

vaporize To destroy something by producing so much heat that it changes from a solid or liquid into vapor (gas).

Index

WEB SITES

http://www.esa.int/esaKIDSen/Cometsandmeteors.html

http://solarsystem.jpl.nasa.gov/planets

http://www.spacetoday.org

http://coolcosmos.ipac.caltech.edu/cosmic_kids/AskKids/asteroids.shtml

http://coolcosmos.ipac.caltech.edu/cosmic_kids/AskKids/comets.shtml

http://www.nasm.si.edu/research/ceps/etp/asteroids

http://neat.jpl.nasa.gov/neofaq.html